GW00673124

THE DO-IT-YOURSELF GUIDE TO FIGHTING THE BIG MOTHERFUCKIN' SAD

ADAM GNADE

PIONEERS PRESS
P.O. Box 8010
Ann Arbor, MI 48107
www.pioneerspress.com

Cover & book design: Rio Safari

ISBN: 978-1-939899-34-7

Printed in the United States of America

First edition: March 2013
Second edition: September 2013
Third edition: May 2014
Fourth edition: November 2014
Fifth edition: March 2015
Sixth edition: February 2016
Seventh edition: February 2017
Eighth edition: September 2018
Ninth edition: April 2019

To Jessie Duke and Bart Schaneman
for teaching me to fight
and Jeff Mangum for "Oh Comely."

Other titles by Adam Gnade:

Hymn California (novel, DutchMoney Books, 2008)

Caveworld (novel, Pioneers Press /Punch Drunk Press, 2013)

Locust House (novella, Pioneers Press, Three.One.G, 2016)

INTRODUCTION

Sometimes I dream of dissecting my life to make a map of it. In this fantasy, I list what food I eat every day and how tired, or sick, or alive I feel when I wake up in the morning. I bar graph how much booze I drink and I chart how many times a day I brush my teeth. Everything goes in until it's a complete and exhaustive profile of my life.

The reason for this is to find the patterns. There's truth in patterns but it's the kind of truth that's hard to accept—the truth we don't always see because we're not always looking.

I'm not always looking, but I have been lately, and I'm seeing the circular conversations of stress and fatalism and the bad cycles of self-doubt. It's all a product of fear. I'm afraid of tomorrow and I'm afraid of next week and I'm afraid that each choice I make will be the one I'll look back on and regret forever.

In high school I was terrified of going anywhere people might not want me to be. I was afraid that what I had to offer wasn't enough for people. I lost all of my friends that way. I'd get a call from somebody and they would say, "You wanna do [whatever] today?" and I'd make an excuse and back out. Without fail.

After a while they'd stop asking and I'd lie in bed imagining all the things people were doing without me, and my mind would loop an endless spiral of, "You...stupid...coward," hours of it, hours until I was tied up in knots. By junior year I ate lunch alone in a far corner of the school. I wanted to die. I wanted to unexist myself. It was a hard year. It got worse.

Life's a shit-business sometimes but you have to drag yourself out of bed and fight, and when you learn *how* to fight a lot of this gets easier. These days I know by name the things that bring me down and I have a box of tools to deal with them. When it's good, I know I'm not a creep and I know I'm not a loser, and when it gets bad—and it *does*—I can remember how the good days felt. Still, there are some mean bastards and some cold fucking facts, and some days it's a willful act of refusal just to keep moving. And there it is, the Big Motherfuckin' Sad comin' at you, and you gotta look it right in the eye and square up to it.

Sometimes life flattens you like a fucking beer can but you can't let it overwhelm you. Like Sean Tillman once sang, "I'll dance on your grave and know that I'm okay." You gotta dance to kill sometimes. Dance until it's just you and the people you love and dance until you have the life you've always wanted.

We're all braver and stronger than we give ourselves credit for. Some days can be a goddamn *bear* but some are good and right and sweet. So, hello, my name is Adam Gnade and here are some pep-talks I've given myself lately. I hope you get something good from them...

DIY GUIDE TO NAVIGATING YOUTH WITHOUT GOING BITTER

1) Never work a job where the bosses don't respect you. Never be afraid to say, "Fuck it," and quit your job, even if the economy is shitty. A bad boss will ruin your life and make you bitter. An abusive boss will make you feel inhuman.

2) Set your expectations high but be ready to work. Be ready to fight like a wild animal.

3) Be good to people. Even the shitty ones. Let the assholes be assholes. You'll sleep better.

4) Never lie. Even when the truth is painful, tell it. Square up to the repercussions.

5) Find good heroes, the ones who make you feel less alone. That being said: Learn how to spend time alone. Too many friends will cheapen your friendships. Find the best people and stick with them. Use this idea: Less friends; better friends. Know that the best people are quiet and brave. The best people listen and the best people know how to do things. To be great, fill yourself up until you're full.

6) Do it (all) yourself. Don't wait around for record labels or publishers or bosses or moneypeople. If you wait to be discovered, you'll wind up disappointed.

7) Freedom is everything.

GUIDE TO NOT FREAKING OUT ALL THE TIME

1) There's a difference between thinking it over and over-thinking it.

2) A few things won't feel better in the morning, but most will. Sometimes the best option is to say, "Fuck those assholes," and sleep on it. When you wake up: *hit back*.

3) You will be scattered and off-balance when you're not doing what your heart tells you to do.

4) If you're feeling marginalized, frustrated, or fucked-over: Take comfort, you're in good company. I've got your back and so do a lot of good folks you haven't met yet. Some people get through

life clean but the rest of us are pulled through the ringer on a daily basis. You're not alone.

5) No matter how beat-up you feel, you are at your best when you're fighting.

FIGHT EVERY DAY

Fight the critics. Fight the bank. Fight your creditors. Fight dismissiveness. Fight the publishers. Fight the agents. Fight fake friends. Fight the scene, the schmoozers, the phonies. Fight the lawyers. Fight the insurance companies. Fight sleep. Fight the neighbors. Fight the weather. Fight short attention spans. Fight the heat. Fight the drought. Fight time. Fight the recession. Fight the unkind. Fight the Internet. Fight the past. Fight the dream-killers. Fight shit-talkers. Fight the morality police. Fight disinterest. Fight sickness. Fight boredom. Fight genetics. Fight preconceptions. Fight the public perception of you. Fight the airlines. Fight the armchair critics. Fight fear. Fight self-doubt. Fight the media. Fight the candidates. Fight not living up to your expectations. Fight bad credit. Fight your car. Fight the bosses. Fight the cowards. Fight irony. Fight laziness. Fight sarcasm. Fight exhaustion. Fight living in the shadow of your heroes. Fight your poverty. Fight your hunger (or don't). Fight the liberals, the conservatives, the Democrats, the Republicans, the anarchists, the Socialists, the Randites, the Tea Partyists, the Communists, the neocons, the plutocrats, the Dixiecrats, the fascists, ET CETERA. Fight the Huns, the Philistines, the Hoard, the Pack. Fight the Great Dumbing Down. Fight hopelessness. Fight rot. Fight traffic. Fight bias. Fight agenda. Fight death. Fight yourself. (And so on.)

DO-IT-YOURSELF GUIDE TO DEALING WITH YOUR CRITICS / THE HATERS

1) Do not, under any circumstances, read the comments. "Anonymous" is not a real person. "Anonymous" is disappointment, weakness fighting back, and envy at its worst. The people who talk shit and complain and stick their nose in your business on the Internet don't hate you; they hate themselves.

2) This is how you win: Surprise everyone with the next thing you do.

3) Don't ever forget the reason you

started doing what you do. When you do forget (and you will, if you get enough attention) find that thing again and get to know it. Have a second honeymoon with the things you once loved.

4) People will always shit on the things they're scared of.

5) There are some fine, intelligent, truthful critics out there. They won't praise, slam, or rage without reason. The rest are failed [fill-in-the-blanks] hurting you because you're doing what they couldn't.

6) Take the place of your heroes. It's okay.

7) Too many good ones are gone. Be the new good ones. And: You'll always have critics, but if you listen to them, we won't always have you.

IN A PLANE ABOVE THE MIDWEST

It's dark and I have my reading light on and it's just me, 4 AM, the red-eye 12:40 out of Portland, everyone asleep in their seats, the cabin rocking to the side with (gentle) turbulence. The plane drops in space and the luggage makes a jostling sound and the engines scream out there in the cold and black. (The seatbelt lights go on...*ding*. What was it Blake sang? "Look at these passengers / If there's babies I'll survive"?)

I'm reading a book, but I'm thinking about my friends back in Portland and I can't keep focused. When you live out in the middle of nowhere and (nearly) everyone you love is off somewhere else, you put a greater importance on the smallest of things: a few minutes in a quiet bar with Dan and Conner and

Lindsey and Ray; meeting Erik in the rain outside Valentine's; Mia playing "Wild Horses" on the bar juke and you think of Jessie crying in Golden Hill, 2004, enough to break your heart. It can be heavy but it's all affirming because you don't get it so often. Which is to say, I'm glad to be headed home because I like how I live, but I'm not sure home will ever be home until all the people I love are there. Of course that's impossible, and if you dwell on it, the longing will drive you crazy.

Maybe that's why people want to go to heaven so bad—all your friends and family (present, past, and beyond) there and accounted for. I know a few things but I don't know about heaven. What I know is this: Life is short and lonely and mean but there are good things that make it worth living. The idea is to grab those things when they show up and hold onto them as long as you can. Of course you can't hold them forever, but what can you hold? Nothing. Life is water through wet cloth. It's all trees and sky passing by a car window, and you can never own any of it, no matter how hard you try and no matter how much you want it. The key is to make your peace with that and have as much fun as you can without hurting anyone. There's no meaning of life but there is meaning and life, and it's there waiting for you. All you need is to open your eyes wide enough to see it when it comes along.

ADAM GNADE

I GOT SOME FRIENDS WHO

1) have seen the world because they goddamn *wanted* to: because their will was that strong.

2) are living their dream because it was theirs to begin with and they see no other way.

3) use words like "purpose" and "exciting" and "adventure" when speaking of their lives. Not "work commute" or "bored to death by my girlfriend" or "because I have to."

4) do exactly what they say they're going to do.

I GOT SOME FRIENDS WHO, PART 2

1) stopped reading once they got an iPhone. (When you're on your deathbed, one thing you'll regret more than most will be the collected months of time you wasted sitting around, pecking at your phone keys.)

2) hate the place they live but refuse to go elsewhere.

3) see their TV screen more than they see the sky.

4) use the words "I'm bored" more than "We should."

5) gave up.

6) are rotting.

7) forgot the dreams they had when their hearts still beat like wild machines.

SUICIDE IS NOT RELIEF

Sometimes it feels like letting go will solve all your problems. The truth is, you can't enjoy relief if you're not alive to feel it. Death is an absence of all; it's not a solution and it won't comfort you or make it feel better. You will be gone. The only pleasure of relief comes from weathering through and seeing the other side. I've been on both sides and the relief after the battle is one of the sweetest things you'll ever feel.

HELPING YOUR FRIENDS GET THROUGH IT

Sometimes the best thing you can do for a friend who's hurting is acknowledge that things get bad and that the bad they feel is just as legitimate as any physical pain. Tell them you understand but don't rush to offer solutions. Don't whitewash it. If you've been there, too, then tell them you've been there. Sometimes "I understand" is the best thing you can say.

DO-IT-YOURSELF GUIDE TO DEALING WITH YOUR CRITICS / THE HATERS, PART 2

1) The best things will always divide opinion.

2) The best things will always be hated by

some, and hate always sounds louder than love. ("Sounds," not "is.")

3) The most ambitious, heartfelt/hard-fought things will always be attacked the hardest. That's the reward for taking chances. (A kid from Nebraska sang this when he was still a kid: "Ambition I've found can lead only to failure / I do not read the reviews / No, I am not singing for you".)

4) Once you start getting attention, don't ever fucking "Google" yourself. Remember what they say about staring into voids.

5) Agenda-based criticism is part of making art like mosquito bites are part of going outdoors.

6) What matters is what you make, not a consumer-based industry's judgment of it. Remember: A judge is gonna judge. Doesn't mean you have to listen.

7) The biggest haters are the ones who are hurting the most. Be kind even if they aren't. Not everyone alive has survived childhood.

DON'T WASTE YOUR TIME

1) with friends you don't love. There's a big difference between "love" and "know."

2) with books you can't give your heart to.

3) with bands that don't write for you. (But beware of bands that sing about "us." Their us is their us. I have my own us and

so do you. See: "Universality and co-opted micro-culture/community as marketing strategy".)

4) with people who are playing you for status or scene cred. Note: Don't schmooze. Ever. Be good to the good of heart. Fuck the rest. You don't need them. Your life is busy as it is. Don't waste your time with creepy fame-vampires.

5) with the bandwagon jumpers.

6) with anyone who doesn't make up their own mind about a cause.

7) with anything that doesn't make you better in its presence.

THE PROS AND CONS OF ANTI-DEPRESSANTS, OR THE TIME I SAW A VISION OF GEORGE W. BUSH THROWING A FOOTBALL AND LIKED IT

There's no shame in trying anti-depressants. They work for some people. For some people they don't. We need to see mental pain like any physical pain. If you break your leg, you get a cast. It's the same with mental distress (or it should be). Anyone who shames you for taking pills to fix a screwed-up brain isn't worthy of being your friend. Just the same: Pay attention to yourself. Know when shit's not working and wean yourself off. Cold turkey will fuck you up heavy. Do the research. Learn how to come off anti-depressants before so much as lowering your dose.

It works differently for everyone.

Some people need a short course of meds to pull them above the water so they can do the heavy lifting on their own. Some people need a full load, for years.

When I took Zoloft, I was dead inside. The sadness and the anxiety went away, but so did everything else. I drank a lot of red wine and I stared at walls and I thought, "Well, I may be a fucking zombified fucking *corpse*, but at least I'm not depressed." The sadness came back, and when it came back and there was nothing left to fight it, I was a shell of myself. I was a husk, skin and bones and no meat inside. It was harrowing, sadness like a goddamn wind, a death-storm in the arctic. It was enough to suffocate all thought and drown out all good things. It howled in my ears and it pressed me into myself and it ached and I froze up inside.

I was on the road then and I slept on

friends' floors and I ruined parties and wasted what could have been a great part of my life.

By the time I got to Brooklyn I knew it was time to quit the pills. Instead of twice daily, I took one every other day. The world was flat. The skyscrapers were one-dimensional, cardboard. They moved in the wind. They were nothing. When it rained, they fell down and turned to pulp.

From New York, Jessie and I drove across country, and then we were in Seattle and we were stuck in an apartment, and then Portland in a basement, and back to San Diego.

In San Diego, I quit Zoloft and within a day my body turned inside-out like a sock. I lay in bed inside Laura's haunted den-room in Clairemont, and I felt my flesh chewed away and saw combinations of numbers and letters flash past my eyes and I knew I was dying. In my head I wrote my will, but there was nothing—a beat-up gray Volvo and a broken laptop and a pile of trash in storage. The ruins of my life.

As it got worse I began to see a vision of George W. Bush in a powder blue Nike tracksuit throwing a football over and over again like some kind of evil, masochistic animated GIF. The weird part is, it was the only thing that was of any comfort. When I'd start to slip away, there was G.W., and I'd come right back.

And that's when I knew I'd gone too far. That kill-crazy fratboy I voted so passionately against was comforting. Yes, indeed—godlike, a father figure, safe, newly re-elected and securely ON MY SIDE. I'd done a twisted 180. I'd flipped, cracked. Dubya and his benevolent football toss looping through my head made me rotten like an apple. I was wormy.

At some point, in an odd moment of clarity, it all made sense and I pulled myself out of bed and asked for help. A friend had an old Zoloft prescription and I went back on it, and the next day I felt better. After that I was smart about it. I weaned myself off for months and when I finally quit again, I was okay. Not out-of-the-woods okay, but the President was gone and so was the pain, and that was good enough. It was a start and you don't get anywhere without a start.

A ROUGH GUIDE TO SURVIVING THE UNSURVIVABLE

1) If you live with monsters you'll become monstrous. This can be good and it can be bad. You need to keep your perspective

and know when it's time to quit a bad scene.

2) Learn the difference between honesty and being a dick.

3) Once you stop looking for identity, you start to die.

4) Don't sabotage yourself. There are enough people out there who'll do it for you. Don't let the assholes win.

5) Read more than you drink.

6) When you feel the Big Motherfuckin' Sad coming on, scream as loudly as you possibly can. It's good medicine.

7) Remember: If someone is talking shit about someone else to you, they probably

talk shit about you, too. If they're doing it on the Internet, they're probably someone you don't want to be friends with. Know a vendetta when you see one. Shit-talkers are like black mold: They'll infect you and you might not even know it. You don't need that darkness in your life. Bitterness will jump from them to you.

NO LAWS BUT YOUR OWN LAWS

1) The smart outlaw is the free outlaw. The free outlaw is the only outlaw.

2) Misbehave passionately.

3) Most cops aren't heroes.

4) Be good to good people. Be good to all animals. You'll know your enemies when you meet them.

5) If you're going to be a savage, be a noble savage. Of course, the definition of nobility you follow should be your own.

6) You will break every rule you set for yourself at least once. No one's word is law because there are no laws.

7) A healthy and free life is the goal of the outlaw.

EVER
GOO
NECES

YONE
D IS
SARY.

YOU NEED TO PUSH HEAVY

This month has been one hell-grade heartbreaker after the next. You roll quietly and deeply long enough and you start to dismantle. (I can feel the ropes unravel, the loosening, which sounds like a slither.) First you stop picking up clothes off the floor. A sweater here. A sock there. You forget about bills and you forget to say "goodnight" and "thanks" and "god bless you." While outside the tall grass grows taller and upstairs your pal on the CD sings, "You aaare the blood flowin' through my *fingers*." This is how you give up in small measures until you give up for real. I need some *fightin'* tools. I'm looking for books that give you truth so fast and hard that you feel cored-out inside and loose and smiley and clean. I'm looking for distractions, easy laughs, encoded hope, life-enrichers, something big and hardy and true. I'm looking everywhere and I believe in that. Which is to say I believe in the potential, if not the outcome. But fuck what comes out; I'm willing to push until the fireworks. And you need to push heavy. So push *heavy*...

LISTEN TO THE CALL OF THE WILD WHEN YOU HEAR IT, OR SEVEN THINGS TO KEEP IN MIND WHEN THE BIG MOTHERFUCKIN' SAD HITS, OR MY NAME IS ADAM GNADE AND THIS IS WHAT I LEARNED ON MY BULLSHIT SPRING VACATION

1) Everyone good is necessary.

2) There are wonderful things disappearing right now. Go find them before they're gone.

3) The "prophets" you meet will let you down. Most artists are politicians. Most politicians think they're artists. Bands everywhere are lying to you right this minute. Find the truth-sayers and stick with them forever.

4) Build your family—in whatever shape it may come.

5) Life isn't dark if you don't want it to be. Wishful thinking and realism are not mutually exclusive.

6) Sing for your supper. You'll respect yourself in the morning.

7) When you hear the call of the wild, you need to run to it.

ADAM GNADE

FIND THE LIFE YOU WANT AND THEN FIGHT UNTIL IT'S YOURS

1) Fighting and loving are the two best things. The worst things are innumerable and will savagely fuck you up if given the chance.

2) No mercy for the dreamkillers.

3) If you're not grappling with self-doubt half the time, you've probably lost perspective. The confident ones give us the worst and most lifeless bullshit.

4) Don't waste your life in front of a screen. If given the choice, avoid any kind of prison. Especially the ones we put ourselves in. Friends don't let friends wilt away on the Internet. Friends open doors and say, "Hey, you wanna get out of here?"

5) The meanest of all is time. Treat the rest accordingly.

6) It's not about the money. Stuff will work out if you work hard. Trust your gut and make the choices you're afraid of. Don't believe them when they tell you to "follow the money." They say that shit because they're scared of losing security. Fuck security. Give us the mess. Give us the big splash of life and color and failure. It's beautiful.

7) You were probably right the first time.

DIY GUIDE TO KILLING OFF ALL BOREDOM

Go outside. Scream your name into The Void. Sit in the sun and feel godlike. Cook a nine-course meal for your friends. Ride a train. Ride a bus. Smash something important. Climb a tree and read a book. WRITE a book. Be sweet to a baby and let them know all big people aren't a) dead inside, b) angry, or c) afraid of adventure. Make your own everything. Stay up all night and walk around the city alone. Learn that you can be a patriot for the land while still hating the government (be a patriot for the deserts, the plains, the mountains, the buffalo, for Woody Guthrie and Frederick Douglass, for 250 years of good books). Find the best genius, which is the genius that speaks plainly. Grow something from a seed. Talk to a dog. Go visit a friend and throw your knife into a river. Sing. Sleep in. Quit your job. Make a zine. Start a war within yourself. Destroy all uncandid thought. Open your heart to the sky. Live.

A GUIDE TO HAPPIER, FREER, LAWLESS LIVING: AN APPLICABLE, REAL-WORLD SOLUTION TO THE QUESTIONS PRESENTED BY "NO BOSSES, NO MASTERS" IDEOLOGY

If you read the type of stuff a lot of my friends read (anarchist theory, CrimethInc, the Situationists, *et al*) you'll hear all kinds of pumped-up, inspiring rhetoric about how you should quit your job and not have bosses and be an "ex-worker." That's fine, but no one ever tells you what to do next. Reading *Days of War, Nights of Love* and Raoul Vaneigem got me fired up and I did quit my job and I did pledge to live lawlessly, but then, "Yeah, but how do I *survive*?" Not everyone is the dumpster-diving type. Not everyone wants to squat or steal. I don't even dress punk, much less identify with the

ADAM GNADE

subculture. I wanted my own version of free.

Unless you come from money, most of us have to work to earn a living. This is no anarchist, post-civ utopia we're living in. This is now, today, and there are certain rules you either ignore, follow, or look for loopholes out of.

The goal for people like me is this: run your own business. Whatever it is: an Etsy craft company, a bookstore, an organic farm, a zine publishing house, you as a freelance writer, as a carpenter for hire, as a screenprinter or a movie-maker...figure out what you want to do and then come up with a plan to do it.

The bulk of my money comes from writing books and zines. I work on them all the time and I stay prolific enough to pay my rent. You have to stick with it and be persistent if you want to live like this.

Slacking off is not an option.

Whatever you choose to do, start small and make your money on your own terms. If you have to work a shitty job while getting your dream off the ground, do that, but get the wheels in motion now and let it build up naturally and be smart about it. Working a shit job won't crush your soul if it's a means to an end and you know what that end is.

Of course there are one-in-a-million dream jobs out there, and some people will make money by singing a tune so seductive that the world will buy into it and feed them forever. That's not something to depend on. You can't wait for a fantasy.

The best way to live is beholden to no man. Be your own boss and figure out the thing you love best and scheme until you have a ground plan. After that, work as ethically as possible and don't fuck over anyone in the process. Look at people who've made it on their own (respectable) terms and learn from what they've built up. It'll be hard, but you'll feel better about yourself at the end of the day. The combination of hard work, extreme diligence, and strong, smart decisions does not fail. Slip up in any of those three and that's when things go south. You won't make it happen if you're sleeping in or doing a bunch of cocaine or working with people who steal from you. Stay on top of it and your dreams will come true. They might not be the dreams you set out with, but you need to remember that dreams change. Just make sure you're happy with what you get. If you're not, go back to the drawing board.

A ROUGH GUIDE TO SURVIVING THE UNSURVIVABLE, PART 2

1) Your heart needs to race every day or else you go stagnant.

2) Feel the earth beneath your feet. Let the concrete crumble.

3) We all need a place to be alone. Stick with crowds too often and you'll lose sight of yourself.

4) Once you stop laughing, it's all over.

5) Obey desire.

6) The greatest thing you can say is this: "I'm still alive."

7) One day we'll all be dead and there's

nothing worse than that. It gets hard and it gets sad. *Push through.*

HAVING BAD HEROES IS LIKE HAVING BAD PARENTS

It'll fuck you up just as much. Who are your heroes? Are they helping you or hurting you? Are you screwing yourself by looking up to the wrong people? Will you fall down in their shadow? What will you do with the good things they gave you? What if they've given you nothing but style and (romantic) nihilism?

TRY OUT ALL YOUR TRICKS UNTIL YOU THRIVE

In Chicago now. Chicago gives me dreams of going back to the city and trying it on.

All the industry and brick, the movement and the shades of gray. I love life in the country but sometimes the city makes sense, and when it does I feel at home.

Walking through Chicago today, I heard lines from Sufjan's record ("Are you writing from the heart?") and I heard parts of *Burn Collector* zines and *Hit It Or Quit It* zines and Saul Bellow: "I am an American, Chicago born—Chicago, that somber city—and go at things as I have taught myself, free-style, and will make the record in my own way: first to knock, first admitted; sometimes an innocent knock, sometimes a not so innocent." Chicago, all the people hustling by in their coats and scarves, red-faced, squinting up at the skyscrapers and the strip of blue sky above. I won't lie, it gets to me. It hits me someplace I'm not usually hit.

ADAM GNADE

Which is no knock on the country life (I need wide open spaces and I need to be left alone to work), but whenever I come to Chicago part of me falls in love, part of me that's more naïve and optimistic than I'd like to admit.

Maybe it's biological—adaptation and the fightin' instinct. Adaptation because in a new environment you must try out all your tricks until you thrive. Root directive: Deal with the new landscape and changing terrain. Plan of attack: Adapt until you flourish; confront all obstacles presented until there's something new. Push forward. Push until it breaks open and shows the golden yolk. Push until you're walking in the clear, the wind in your face, a clean path before you…

THE DO-IT-YOURSELF GUIDE TO MEETING GOOD PEOPLE AND FINDING NEW FRIENDS

As someone who spends a lot of time alone, I know how hard it is to make friends. Sometimes it might not seem worth the risk, but remember, you can't sail a boat without a crew, and boats are fucking cool. One thing people overlook is that friends can be anywhere. They don't have to have the same diet or music taste or politics as you. They don't have to be your age or your color or your class. The hardest thing is to overcome your anxiety and reach out, but if you do (and if that person is worth a damn) they'll respect your courage, because if there's one thing good people love, it's bravery. Making friends can be one of the scariest fucking things you'll ever do, but once you have them they'll help soothe that fear. We can make it alone but it's better (and more fun) not to.

HOW TO FEEL ALIVE FOR THE PRICE OF A MATCH

I've been building a fire every night when the work is done. Outside, late, under these big fucking MOONS we've been having. You know that feeling you get when you stare into the embers of a campfire and all this primordial QUIET comes over you and you feel so strong and calm and purposeful? Maybe you have a jug of wine. Maybe a knife to sharpen. (A book and a flashlight?) And there's that crackling fire and the moon all blood-orange-glowing in the eastern sky and you can hear crickets in the bar-ditch and the freight-trains down by the

Missouri River. That's how you feel alive...well, one way at least. You need to make a list of them for when you need it the most. Start now.

ONE THING I'VE LEARNED FROM THE FARMERS AROUND HERE

Some things make you stronger. Some just make you old.

WARNING: IF YOU TRY TO CREATE SOMETHING "DIFFERENT"

1) You will feel so alone sometimes it will be harrowing. You will be broke while your friends with steady (safe) jobs eat well and go to the movies and buy nice clothes and take vacations. (You won't get vacation time but you'll travel more than anyone you know. Sometimes you'll be on

the road so much you won't remember the way home. Don't be afraid to ask for directions.)

2) You'll make money in vast, jerking convulsions and then you won't see any for a long time. You'll be hungry. You'll get angry. You'll get goddamn furious. You'll want to pack it in. You'll rethink everything and decide to "quit" or "drop out of society" or "disappear forever." And you'll do this at least once a day. But you'll stick around because some part of you has always believed.

3) Your heart will break and your mind will change inwardly and you will grow inside in tangles and curving passageways while the rest go dry and wither and blow away. You will learn every day.

4) You will sleep well and you will hold your head high. You'll see what the rest do and you'll know you are on the edge of something tall and dark and strange.

5) You will never be bored. You will never be, like, "Uh, I dunno, what do you wanna do?"

6) You will have things you've made and holding these things in your hand will make your heart swell.

7) You will be free.

A SEVEN-POINT LIFE PLAN

1) BENEVOLENCE Pledge to be benevolent, moral, and honest in the midst of online shit-talkers, surface thinkers, and secret capitalists. Be noble

while the hate flows forth.

2) TURN OFF YOUR COMPUTER You won't find what you need on the Internet.

3) SUICIDE IS NOT PAINLESS The feelings you have are the feelings we all have. Let's fight together. Here: gnadegnadegnade@gmail.com. Any time. I'm here.

4) YOU'RE AS STRONG AND AS READY AS YOU WANT For years I let people tell me I was useless, that I couldn't make any decisions for myself and that I couldn't fix or build or create anything substantial. Living out here on the farm, I've been forced to push myself, and I've learned I'm a lot more capable than I was lead to believe. Fuck the unbelievers in your life. You're as strong and as ready as you want.

5) YOUR LIFE, THE MOVIE This line always gets me: "If your life was a movie, would you want to watch it?" I'd like to say yes, but a lot of the time I can't. And when I can't, I feel like a goddamn bomb about to explode. Can you say yes? Ask yourself that right now and if you don't like the answer do something about it.

6) TAKING YOURSELF TOO SERIOUSLY FOR TOO LONG WILL HAVE THE OPPOSITE EFFECT ON EVERYONE ELSE I'm all for believing in what we do. I believe in work and self-seriousness and the quiet power of confidence and resolve. I believe in pushing for the thing you love until the fucking doors creak and break and smash inward with a great cloud of splinters and dust. But you need to know when to step back and have a laugh at your own expense and lose your

driven fucking attitude for a while. A little pressure let off is a good thing. Taking yourself too seriously for too long will have the opposite effect on everyone else.

7) WHEN THE SAD STARTS TO HIT
Open the door, leave the house, walk. It helps. Also, ask for help. It might be the bravest thing you'll ever do. Sometimes we all need to reach for a light switch in the dark.

YOUR FRIENDS WILL CARRY YOU HOME

Driving here at dusk is a revelation. The tawny hills and old farmhouses. The frozen creek and grain silos. Sometimes, when the light is good, I feel like I could drive off the bridge over the Missouri and down into the blue and walk off just fine.

On days like this you feel indestructible—a thing made up of motion and potency, an undying island. But of course you're not. One bad patch of ice and you're done. It's tragedy and super-miracle, the big truth besides life itself: The end will come for you like it came for everyone else. But if you think like that you'll stay inside forever. Shake it off. Move forward. Keep driving...

Winter is here and it's cold and sun-lit and beautiful. Driving alone today I saw the countryside golden and freezing. At noon the fields were rich yellow and the sky cloudless and blue and smoky (smoke from what? Chimneys and meth shacks? Trash fires on farms?). All summer I drove and listened to country records that felt like the place I was in. Merle, Kitty Wells, Phosphorescent, Damon Moon, Roy Acuff. In the fall I wanted

NOISE to stir up my guts and I wanted the white-roar to drown out my thoughts after working on the book all day. (Like Hemingway says, after you're done writing for the day, you need to forget the story and let your subconscious work out the kinks). Now I drive quietly and I think and I plot. There are no hard and fast answers. I know this. But it doesn't stop me from asking.

At home on the farm, I sit in my freezing room upstairs under all the blankets and I read. (Like Bart told me in a letter, this coming year will be "the year of re-reading.") This week, it's endless back issues of *Harper's* and *The New Yorker*. It's Melville (all night until I fall asleep with the book in my hands), Faulkner, Carver, Dostoevsky, Didion, Cather, García Márquez, Langston Hughes, Thomas Jefferson…all the tricks

I'll need when it's time to move on and write the next one. Training. Or retraining.

I'll be honest with you: I could give up everything and read all day. Leave me with a bottle of red wine (Spanish, *Rioja*, *Jumilla*) and some blueberries and a stack of books and I'll lose myself and let my beard grow (badly) and be done with it. I want adventure and I want to sail across the sea, but give me a good book and I'll let my hours sink into nothing but ideas and characters and STORY.

I'm not a social person. I try to find compassion and believe in people, but the more people I meet the more I hate humans. Just the same—and because people show me how mean and boring and frivolous we are—there are a select few, a small number (maybe you're one of them) who inspire me to keep moving and make me realize that the best part of all this vicious, meatgrinding destitution is who you choose to spend time with.

I'm going to level with you here: I try to be optimistic, but there are days when I see the promised land and the promised land—the big golden sunflash—isn't god and it isn't heaven or enlightened solace, it's death as relief, an end to the mindnumbing bullshit and the fear and the ridiculous days sitting around your fucking bedroom thinking, "*This is it?* All this struggling and a fast path to old age? The body that falls apart no matter how strong or sweet or goodhearted you are, no matter how hard you love the people in your life? The base *emptiness* at the end? If this is *it* I want my money back." And I could *take* my money back. We're fragile. It's easy. Just a left when you should go right. A choice—a big choice—and the thundering blackness as consequence. I can make those decisions and make them final.

But I'm here. I choose to stay here because I'm given reasons. Now, a lot of those reasons are mine, they're private reasons, but here's a reason I'll share: the good people. The ones closest to my heart are the people who show me how to fight and remind me that there's an option that outweighs the coward's path. You can be a hermit and you can be an island, but when the paint gets stripped away, we are what we build up around us. We are the sum of our actions, our chosen environment, our loves, our pleasures.

So, count on your friends. Have faith in your friends. Never let them forget that sometimes—in the worst, darkest, most fucked moments when the whole gale is howling around you—they are what keeps you here—alive and fighting. Your friends will be your ballast. Your friends will sing your story when there's no one left to know the tune. Fuck the ones who aren't worth a damn; your true friends are the answer you're looking for. Your friends will carry you home.

EPILOGUE

It's fall again. The leaves are turning orange and the sky is open and blue and endless. There's a big good world out there and you deserve every piece of it you can grab. Whether alone or with people, you need to go start some shit. Throw back the covers. Get out of bed, take a shower, and eat a good meal. Then open the door and step outside. I'm right there with you.

ABOUT THE AUTHOR

Adam Gnade's (*guh nah dee*) work is released as a series of books and records that share characters and themes; the fiction writing continuing plot-lines left open by the self-described "talking songs" in an attempt to compile a vast, detailed, interconnected, personal history of contemporary American life. This is his first published work of nonfiction.